KENAI TRAILS

A GUIDE TO THE OUTSTANDING
WILDLAND TRAILS OF
ALASKA'S KENAI PENINSULA

ALASKA NATURAL HISTORY ASSOCIATION
2004

For me, and for thousands with similar inclinations, the most important passion of life is the overpowering desire to escape periodically from the clutches of a mechanistic civilization. To us the enjoyment of solitude, complete independence, and the beauty of undefiled panoramas is absolutely essential to happiness.

–Bob Marshall

Designer: Carole Thickstun
Illustrations/Maps: Lawrence Ormsby
Editor: Nora Deans
Project Manager: Lisa Oakley
Contributors and Agency Coordinators: Lezlie Murray, Chugach National Forest; Jack Sinclair, Alaska State Parks; Sandy Brue, Kenai Fjords National Park; Candace Ward, Kenai National Wildlife Refuge

Alaska Natural History ASSOCIATION

750 West Second Avenue, Suite 100
Anchorage, AK 99501
www.alaskanha.org

Alaska Natural History Association is a nonprofit publisher of books and other materials about Alaska's public lands. For more information or to join: *www.alaskanha.org*

ISBN 0-930931-24-6
Printed in China

Contents

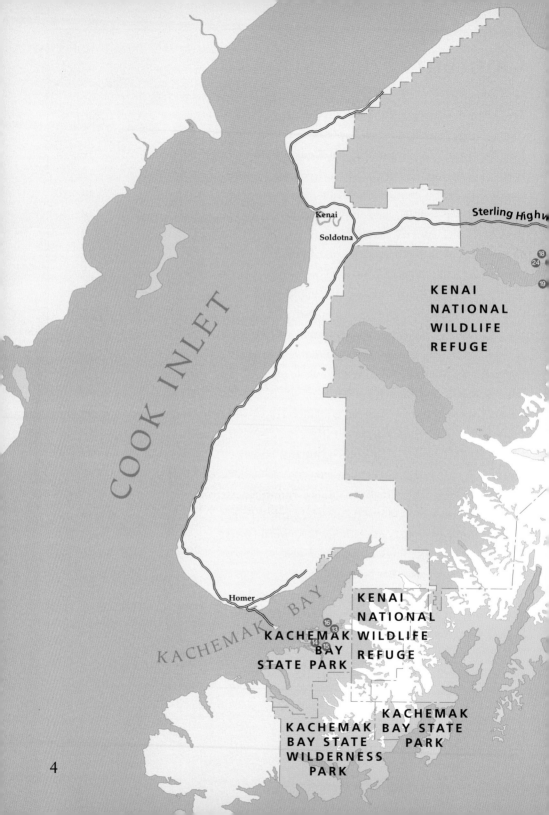

COOK INLET

Sterling Highw

Kenai

Soldotna

**KENAI
NATIONAL
WILDLIFE
REFUGE**

18
24
19

KACHEMAK BAY

Homer

16
13
14
15

**KACHEMAK
BAY
STATE PARK**

**KENAI
NATIONAL
WILDLIFE
REFUGE**

**KACHEMAK
BAY STATE
PARK**

**KACHEMAK
BAY STATE
WILDERNESS
PARK**

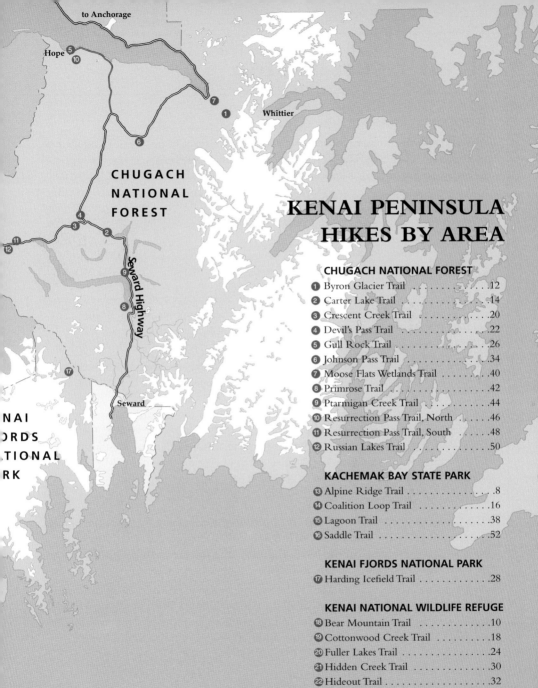

KENAI PENINSULA
HIKES BY AREA

Trail Users Guide

WELCOME

Alaska is known the world over as a special place of great beauty beckoning to those seeking high adventure. The Kenai Peninsula south of Anchorage is one such place. Its highways provide great jumping-off points to the backcountry. Kenai pathways lead to remote lakes, grinding glaciers, deep-green forests, and some of the world's most outstanding wildlife. The Forest Service, the U.S. Fish and Wildlife Service, the National Park Service and Alaska State Parks welcome you to more than 300 miles of trails.

HOW TO USE THIS GUIDE

We have attempted to put as much information about each trail as possible on every page, including length, difficulty, and other recreational opportunities—fishing, cross-country skiing, snowshoeing, mountain biking, dogsledding or horseback riding. Availability of cabins and accessibility to people with disabilities are also included.

The abbreviation "MP" has been used for physical mileposts along the Seward and Sterling highways. The Seward Highway connects Anchorage and Seward, and physical mileposts along the highway begin at Seward (MP 0) and end at Anchorage (MP 127). The Sterling Highway begins at its junction with the Seward Highway at Tern Lake on the Kenai Peninsula and ends at Homer. Physical mileposts note the distance from Seward. For example, the Sterling and Seward Highway junction is MP 37.7 of the Sterling Highway (37.7 miles north of Seward). Homer is MP 142.

CHUGACH NATIONAL FOREST

The Chugach National Forest was established in 1907, making it one of the oldest national forests in the United States. It is also one of the most diverse forests with its glacier-filled mountains on the Kenai Peninsula, the marine ecosystem of Prince William Sound, and the vast wetlands of the Copper River Delta.

At 5.4 million acres, the Chugach is the second largest national forest in America. The most westerly and northerly of all the national forests, the Chugach is known for its world-class wildland recreational opportunities and its many fish and wildlife residents. The Forest Service maintains about 200 miles of trails on the Kenai Peninsula.

KENAI FJORDS NATIONAL PARK

Kenai Fjords National Park was formally established in 1978 as a national monument. In 1980, park status was attained through the Alaska National Interest Lands Conservation Act (ANILCA). This spectacular park encompasses a jagged coastal mountain system on the southern Kenai Peninsula, a large portion of the 300-square-mile Harding Icefield, and glacial-carved fjords of great beauty. More than 35 glaciers flow from the Harding Icefield. Some, like the popular Exit Glacier, terminate on land, while others flow to tidewater where they calve and create icebergs—great haul outs for harbor seals. Park animals include moose, bear, bald eagles, sea otters, sea lions, several species of whales, and thousands of seabirds.

KENAI NATIONAL WILDLIFE REFUGE

The Kenai National Wildlife Refuge was originally established as the Kenai National Moose Range in 1941. In 1980, the Alaska National Interest Lands Conservation Act (ANILCA) renamed the refuge and broadened its purpose to conserve all wildlife populations and habitats in their natural diversity. ANILCA also designated 1.35 million acres of the refuge as wilderness. The refuge, at nearly 2 million acres, rises from lowland spruce forests dotted with hundreds of lakes to the snow-capped Kenai Mountains and Harding Icefield. More than 200 miles of waterways and trails lead to exciting salmon and trout fishing, canoe trips, and day hikes to scenic vistas and wildlife viewing opportunities.

KACHEMAK BAY STATE PARK

Kachemak Bay, Alaska's first state park, is approximately 400,000 acres of mountains, glaciers, forests, and ocean. This park is prime habitat for sea life, including sea otters, seals, porpoises, and whales. The park's land animals include moose, black bear, mountain goats, coyotes, and wolves.

Other Kenai Peninsula state parks to explore:

Caines Head State Recreation Area is the site of an abandoned World War II fort, reached by boat or on foot from Seward.

Captain Cook State Recreation Area, located on the coast of Cook Inlet, is a great site for beachcombing tide-swept shores, bird watching, berry picking, and wildlife observation. Stormy Lake offers summer swimming and winter ice fishing. Wildlife includes beluga whales, harbor seals, beaver, muskrats, bald eagles, sandhill cranes, trumpeter swans, arctic and common loons, goldeneye ducks, mergansers, moose, bear, coyotes, and wolves.

Alpine Ridge Trail

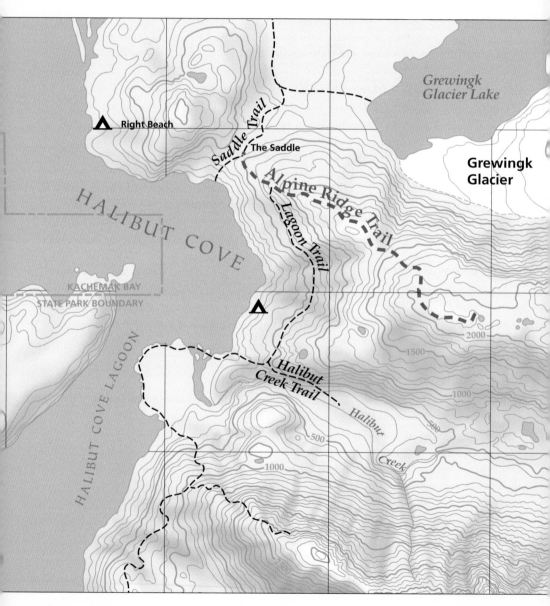

TRAIL INFORMATION

Length One Way: 2.5 miles

Roundtrip Time: 4 hours (timberline)

Recommended Seasons: May–October

Trail End: 2,100 ft. knoll with views of Grewingk Glacier

Map: Nautical Chart #16645, Gore Point to Anchor Point

Difficulty: Difficult

Elevation Gain: 1,650 feet

Condition: Fair

ACCESS

All trail access is by boat or plane. Numerous hazards exist on the bay. Be aware of the tides; trailheads are only accessible during high tide.

WILDLIFE

Land mammals include moose, black bear, mountain goats, coyotes, and wolves. The many species of birds that inhabit the bay include bald eagles, gyrfalcons, and puffins.

DESCRIPTION

Kachemak Bay State Park was Alaska's first, and is roughly 400,000 acres in size. Mountains, glaciers, forests, and ocean are all included within its boundaries.

Kachemak Bay's tides are among the largest in the world. The average vertical difference between high and low waters is 15 feet, with an extreme of 28 feet. Tidal currents can be very strong, and rapids are often created in narrow passages, such as the entrances to Halibut Cove.

Alpine Ridge is a popular, quick route to alpine areas. The trail begins near the high point on the Saddle Trail, steeply follows a ridge through spruce and alder to alpine tundra, and ends on a treeless knoll at an elevation of 2,100 feet. The views are spectacular, encompassing the Grewingk Glacier and a deep glacial valley.

Bear Mountain Trail

0.8 mile   *Kenai National Wildlife Refuge*

HIDD
LAK

Skilak Lake Road

Bear Mountain Trail

Skilak Lake Road

Upper Ohmer Lake

Rock Lake

Hidden Creek Trail

SKILAK WILDLIFE

RECREATION AREA

Skilak Lookout Trail

X 1568'

SKILAK
LAKE

TRAIL INFORMATION

Length One Way: 0.8 mile

Roundtrip Time: 2 hours

Recommended Seasons: All seasons

Trail End: On rock outcropping overlooking the Skilak Lake area

USGS Map: Kenai B-1

Difficulty: Moderate

Elevation Gain: 400 feet

Condition: Trail is short; gains elevation quickly. Good condition

ACCESS

At MP 58 of the Sterling Highway, turn onto the east entrance of Skilak Lake Road. Parking area and trailhead are 6.1 miles down Skilak Lake Road. They are approximately 2.4 miles west of Hidden Lake Campground.

WILDLIFE

Black and brown bears, moose; waterfowl often in Rock Lake at the trailhead.

DESCRIPTION

Bear Mountain is a short trail, and gains elevations quickly. The trail passes through spruce forest at its beginning, but soon opens up to scattered alder patches. Ending at a rock outcrop, the wide panoramic views take in the Kenai Mountains and Skilak Lake. Bring your camera and binoculars. A few areas are suitable for camping on top of Bear Mountain. Please use a backpacking stove to reduce impact. Carry water; water is NOT available along this trail. There are many species of wildflowers growing along the trail throughout the summer. There are no fishing opportunities along this trail. The lake (Rock Lake) across from the Bear Mountain parking area has no sport fish in it. Snowshoeing is good when there is enough snow cover.

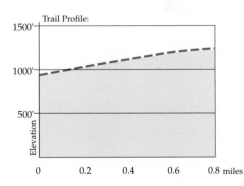

Trail Profile:

Byron Glacier Trail

0.8 mile   *Chugach National Forest*

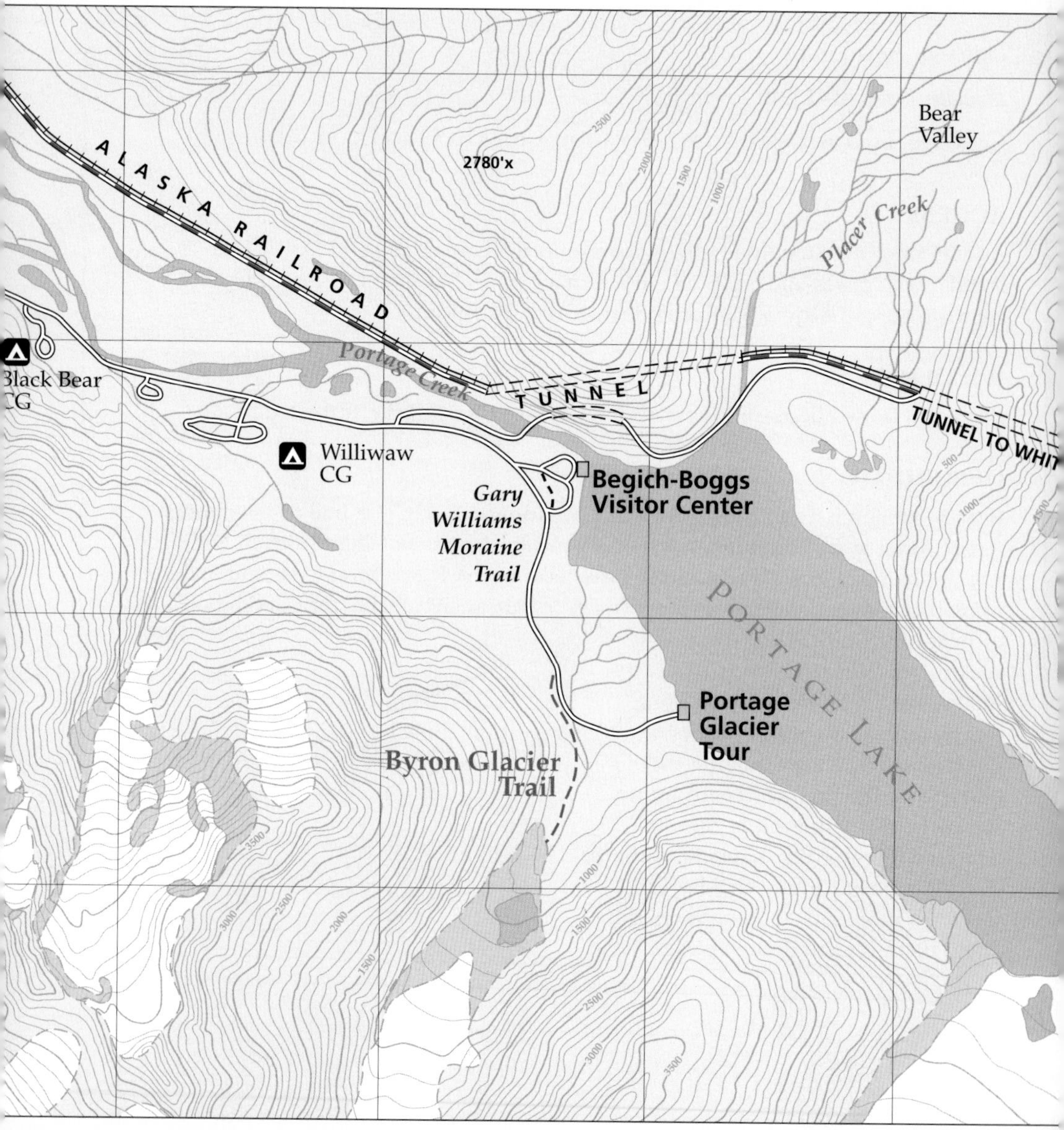

Bear
Valley

Placer Creek

2780'x

ALASKA RAILROAD

Portage Creek

TUNNEL

TUNNEL TO WHIT

Black Bear
CG

Williwaw
CG

Begich-Boggs
Visitor Center

*Gary
Williams
Moraine
Trail*

PORTAGE LAKE

Portage
Glacier
Tour

Byron Glacier
Trail

TRAIL INFORMATION

Length One Way: 0.8 mile

Roundtrip Time: 1–1.5 hours

Recommended Seasons: Mid–summer until the snow flies

Trail End: Snow field at the base of Byron Glacier.

USGS Map: Seward D-5

Difficulty: Moderate

Elevation Gain: 150 feet

Condition: Generally good.

ACCESS

Five miles up the Portage Glacier Highway, turn right at the sign that says "Byron Glacier Trail and Portage Glacier Cruises" and drive one more mile to the Byron Glacier trailhead parking lot.

WILDLIFE.

Moose, black bear, bald eagles, mountain goats, migrating birds, and ice worms on the snowfield near Byron Glacier.

DESCRIPTION

The trail leads to the snow fields at the base of Byron Glacier. The first half of the trail is well-maintained; the second half becomes rocky with small stream crossings and some standing water. Good family trail. Alders, cottonwoods, and ferns along the trail.

SPECIAL CONSIDERATIONS

Due to the steep walls of Byron Valley, the area is highly prone to avalanches. The best time to hike the trail is after the huge cornices that overhang the valley are gone, which is usually in late June or early July, and before heavy snowfalls begin in late autumn. However, avalanches can happen any time of year and are dependent on the very changeable weather in the area.

Carter Lake Trail

3.3 miles   *Chugach National Forest*

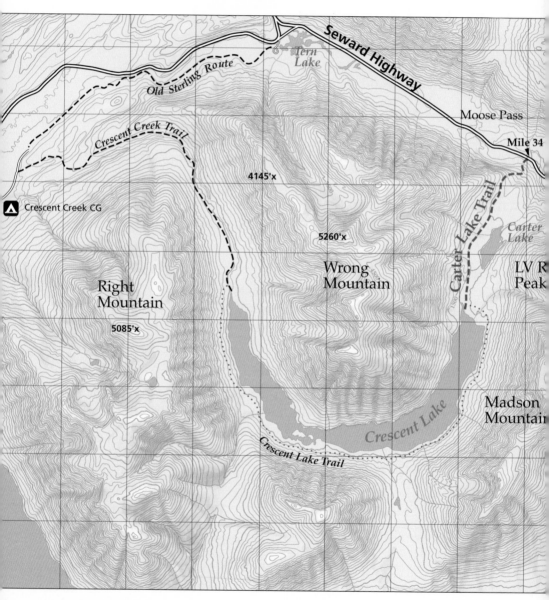

TRAIL INFORMATION

Length One Way: 3.3 miles

Roundtrip Time: 4 hours

Recommended Seasons: All seasons

Trail End: East end of Crescent Lake

USGS Maps: Seward B-7, C-7

Difficulty: More difficult

Elevation Gain: 955 feet

Condition: Well maintained, but
  muddy in places

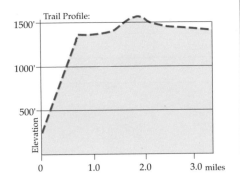

ACCESS

Trailhead is at MP 34 of the Seward Highway. The trail is closed to saddle/pack stock from April 1 to June 30, and motorized vehicles from May 1 to November 30. Bikes are allowed from July 1 to March 31.

WILDLIFE

Moose, black and brown bear, mountain goat, Dall sheep.

DESCRIPTION

An excellent trail for day hiking, the trail rises into subalpine and alpine habitats in only 1.5 miles. After the first section, it levels out, and vegetation changes to subalpine with lower growing shrubs and a multitude of wildflowers.

In summer, it is extremely difficult to access the west end of Crescent Lake on this trail because of a creek crossing during high water, the narrow tread, and tall grass. One section of the creek flowing into Carter Lake is wide and without a bridge, so expect to get wet.

There is good fishing for stocked rainbow trout in Carter Lake. Fishing success varies at the east end of Crescent Lake.

Carter Lake Trail has good winter access for cross-country skiing, snowshoeing, and snowmobiling. The recommended winter route to Crescent Lake public recreation cabins is via Carter Lake Trail and across frozen Crescent Lake, except during extreme avalanche danger periods. Also, you need to check ice conditions on Crescent Lake before winter travel.

Coalition Loop Trail

5.5 miles   *Kachemak Bay State Park*

TRAIL INFORMATION

Length One Way: 5.5 miles

Loop Time: 3 hours

Recommended Seasons: May–October

Trail End: Loop

USGS Maps: Seldovia C-4, C-3, B-4, B-3

Difficulty: Moderate; short steep climbs

Elevation Gain: 400 feet

Condition: Poor–Good

ACCESS

Marine Access–China Poot Bay Trailhead (high tide only); and at mile 0.2 and mile 1.8 of China Poot Lake Trail.

WILDLIFE

Sea otters, seals, porpoise, whales, moose, black bear, mountain goats, coyotes, and wolves. Birds include eagles, gyrfalcons, and puffins.

TRAIL DESCRIPTION

Connecting Halibut Cove Lagoon with China Poot Bay (1.6 miles) and dedicated to the Kachemak Bay Citizen's Coalition, this trail shares some of the 23,000 acres once destined for logging and development, which Alaska State Parks acquired with the help of grass-roots Coalition volunteers. The trail extends in a loop back to China Poot Lake Trail, near the north shore of China Poot Lake. It climbs over a low ridge from mile 0.2 of China Poot Lake Trail and opens to scenic views of China Poot Bay, where bald eagles soar over bluffs. The trail continues south, descending to China Poot Bay (a good stop for lunch or boat pick-up). Just minutes beyond the bay it traverses steep, forested hillsides, then passes through low ridges and valleys—note the few hemlocks in this area. The trail then passes high along China Poot Creek to a spectacular overlook of China Poot Lake (mile 4.0). As the trail descends toward the lakeshore, it rejoins China Poot Lake Trail.

CHINA POOT LAKE TRAIL (2.6 miles) gently climbs 500 feet through the forest and over a low ridge, passing two small lakes where loons are common and blueberries are plentiful (August). The trail meanders through cottonwoods and ends at the China Poot Lake Campsite and inlet stream. This is a great camping or picnic site, and a great departure point for the Poot Peak or Wosnesenski areas.

Cottonwood Creek Trail

2.5 miles   *Kenai National Wildlife Refuge*

Lower Ohmer Lake

Upper Skilak

Frying Pan Island

Caribou Islands

PRIVATE PROPERTY

SKILAK LAKE

Skilak Lake Road

PRIVATE PROPERTY

Cottonwood Creek Trail

500

1000

TRAIL INFORMATION

Length One Way: 2.5 miles

Roundtrip Time: 4 to 6 hours

Recommended Seasons: All seasons

Trail End: At rise above Skilak Lake

USGS Map: Kenai B-1

Difficulty: Difficult

Elevation Gain: about 2,200 feet

Condition: Fair

ACCESS

Accessible only by boat or float plane. The trailhead is on the south shore of Skilak Lake. To find Skilak Lake, turn onto the east entrance of Skilak Lake Road at Sterling Highway MP 58. Travel 8.5 miles to Upper Skilak Lake Campground, and launch your boat from the campground. Cross 3.5 miles of open water on Skilak Lake to trailhead.

WILDLIFE

Dall sheep, bear, marmots, eagles.

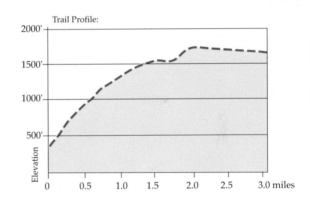

Trail Profile:

DESCRIPTION

Watch for winds when making the lake crossing. Sudden winds can be extreme, making the lake rough and dangerous. IF WINDY, STAY ON THE SHORE. If crossing the lake in winter, check conditions with Refuge Headquarters first.

The trail provides quick access to the alpine habitat above Skilak Lake, with a dramatic transition from spruce to hemlock. Berry picking is good during late summer. Hikers are not restricted to trails in the alpine areas; explore wherever you wish. Spectacular views of Skilak Lake and surrounding mountains open up. The most suitable campsites are above treeline. Firewood is not available, so bring a stove. After the snow melts, there is little or no water available, so carry water. Please respect the privacy and rights of private land owners within the refuge.

The trail is good for snowshoeing, but avoid avalanche areas.

Crescent Creek Trail

6.5 miles   *Chugach National Forest*

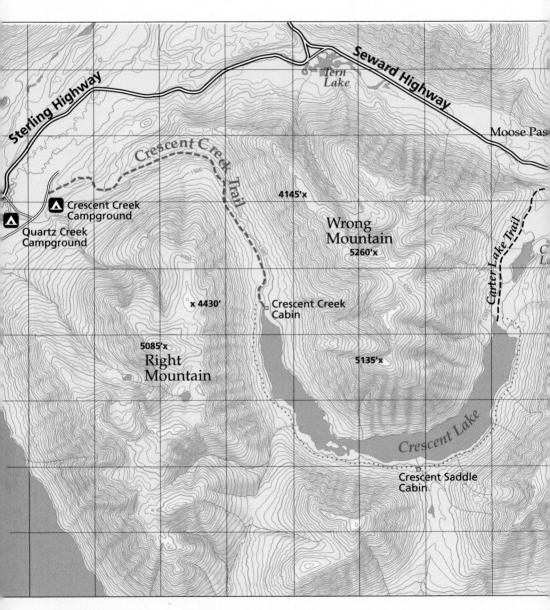

Sterling Highway

Seward Highway

Tern Lake

Moose Pas

Crescent Creek Trail

1500

4145'x

Wrong Mountain

5260'x

Crescent Creek Campground

Quartz Creek Campground

4000

x 4430'

Crescent Creek Cabin

5085'x

Right Mountain

5135'x

Carter Lake Trail

C L

1500

Crescent Lake

Crescent Saddle Cabin

TRAIL INFORMATION

Length One Way: 6.5 miles

Roundtrip Time: 6 to 7 hours

Recommended Seasons: Spring–Fall

Trail End: West shore of Crescent Lake at the Crescent Creek Cabin

USGS Maps: Seward B-7, C-7, and C-8

Difficulty: Easy

Elevation Gain: 1,300 feet

Condition: Well maintained, though sometimes muddy in places

ACCESS

At MP 45 of the Sterling Highway, 7 miles west of the Seward/Sterling Highway junction, turn south on to Quartz Creek Road. Take the left fork. Drive past Quartz Creek and Crescent Creek Campgrounds to trailhead at mile 3.5 of the Quartz Creek Road. Bikes are allowed July 1 to March 31. Trail closed year-round to horses and mountain bikes.

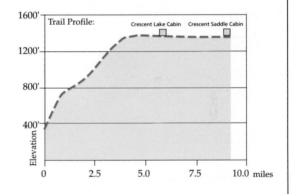

WILDLIFE

Moose, black and brown bear, Dall sheep.

DESCRIPTION

This is an excellent trail for family outings and day hikes. The trail alternates between openings of meadows with wildflowers to forested areas. Long gradual grades follow a small creek upwards through a birch-aspen forest, then the trail drops into scenic Crescent Creek Canyon. Crescent Lake is just below treeline. Most good campsites are near the lake. Hunting is allowed in designated seasons. Fishing for trophy-size grayling is best in the west half of Crescent Lake. Grayling are also in Crescent Creek.

There is extreme avalanche danger on the trail in winter and early spring. For winter access to Crescent Lake Cabin, use Carter Lake Trail and traverse across frozen Crescent Lake, except during periods of extreme avalanche danger. Trail is closed to saddle-pack stock from April 1 to June 30 and motorized vehicles from May 1 to November 30.

Note: the trail from Crescent Lake Cabin to Crescent Saddle Cabin along Crescent Lake is very difficult and is only used in early summer and early fall.

Devil's Pass Trail

10 miles *Chugach National Forest*

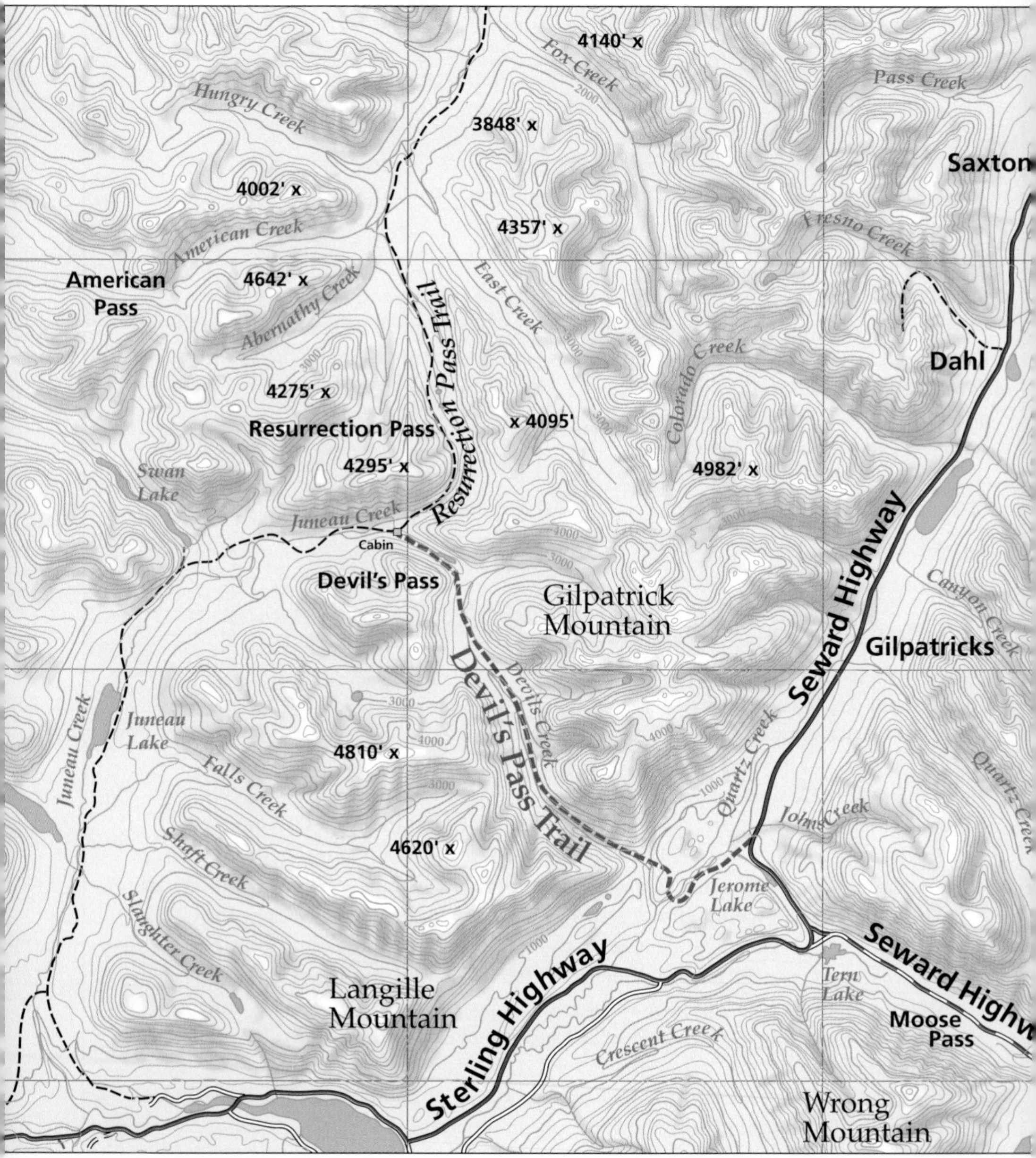

TRAIL INFORMATION

Length One Way: 10 miles

Roundtrip Time: 10-12 hours

Recommended Seasons: Spring-Fall

Trail End: Just past Devils Pass, at intersection with Resurrection Trail

USGS Maps: Seward C-7, C-8

Difficulty: More difficult

Elevation Gain: 1,400 feet

Condition: Good

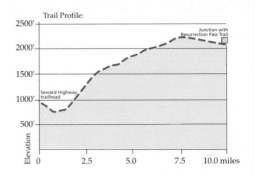

ACCESS
The trailhead is on the west side of the Seward Highway at Mile 39. The trail is closed to saddle/pack stock from April 1 to June 30, and motorized vehicles from February 16 to November 30. Bikes are allowed July 1 to March 31. Snowmobiles (unless for subsistence) are not allowed at anytime on the first two miles. Beyond mile 2, they are allowed from December 1 to February 15.

WILDLIFE
Moose, caribou, wolves, wolverine, ptarmigan, grouse, marmot.

DESCRIPTION
The trail accesses seldom-traveled alpine valleys—all excellent for cross-country hiking. Spruce-birch forests at lower elevations grade into tundra with wildflowers. A variety of scenery abounds—mountains, forests, streams, lakes and alpine areas.

The trail connects to Resurrection Pass Trail for extended trips. You can take a two-day trip with camping at Beaver Point tent site (2 miles from trailhead) or Devil's Pass public recreation cabin, located 10 miles from trailhead above treeline. No camping spots from miles 2-8. Along the trail, reddish-gray trees killed by spruce bark beetle are now a fire danger. Use caution with bear and moose. You can fish for Dolly Varden in Devil's Pass Lake. Hunting is permitted in season.

Winter travel is unsafe and not recommended because of the extreme avalanche hazard beyond mile 3. Be prepared for rapid weather changes.

Fuller Lakes Trail

TRAIL INFORMATION

Length One Way: 2.9 miles

Roundtrip Time: 4 to 6 hours

Recommended Seasons: All seasons

Trail End: Fuller Lakes

USGS Maps: Kenai B-1, C-1

Difficulty: Strenuous

Elevation Gain: 1,400 feet

Condition: Good, with muddy
  spots

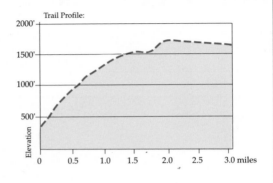

Trail Profile:

ACCESS

The Fuller Lakes Trail begins at MP 57 of the Sterling Highway.

WILDLIFE

Moose, black and brown bear, Dall sheep, beaver, ptarmigan, grouse, songbirds.

DESCRIPTION

Fuller Lakes Trail provides access to the Mystery Creek Unit of the Kenai Wilderness. From Lower Fuller Lake, the trail proceeds through scattered stands of dwarf willow and birch. You'll have excellent views of the Kenai Mountains along the trail, and you can fish for grayling in Lower Fuller Lake. There are several campsite possibilities between the upper and lower lakes. Off-trail camping is also possible. Off-trail hiking is relatively easy in the Upper Fuller Lake area. Trips to nearby ridges provide spectacular views—and a steep climb! You can fish for Dolly Varden in Upper Fuller Lake, and berry pick-ing is good in late summer. Wood is limited near Upper Fuller Lake, so please do not build fires in this area. Keep in mind minimum-impact camping techniques. Sturdy hiking boots are recommended. There is good skiing and snowshoeing in winter if snow cover is adequate.

Gull Rock Trail

5.1 miles   *Chugach National Forest*

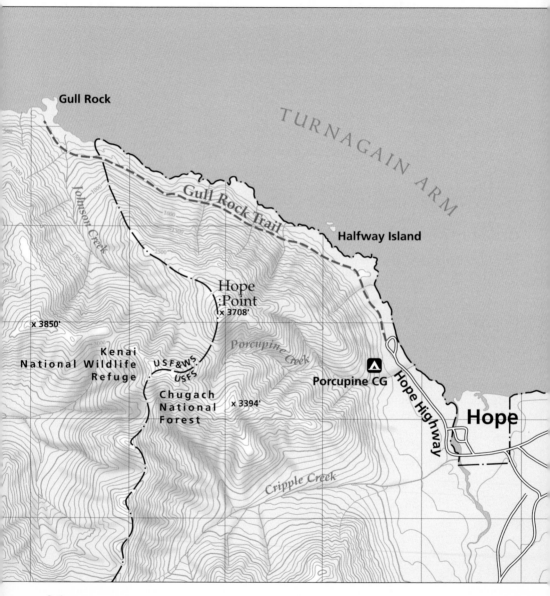

TRAIL INFORMATION

Length One Way: 5.1 miles

Roundtrip Time: 6 hours

Recommended Seasons: May–October

Trail End: Gull Rock

USGS Map: Seward D-8

Difficulty: Easy

Elevation Gain: 620 feet

Condition: Excellent

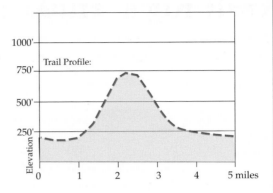

Trail Profile:

ACCESS

At MP 56.5 of the Seward Highway, turn west onto Hope Highway. Drive 17.5 miles to Porcupine Campground, west of Hope. Trail starts at the far northwest end of the campground. Trail is closed to saddle/pack stock from April 1–June 30 and to motorized vehicles from May 1–November 30. Bikes are allowed from July 1 to March 31.

WILDLIFE

Moose, black and brown bear, beluga whales, many birds.

DESCRIPTION

An excellent family day hike, with long gradual grades and a well-maintained trail, although muddy in places with some downed trees. The trail follows an old wagon train road. Look for old sawmill, cabin, and stable near Johnson Creek. Very scenic views as it parallels Turnagain Arm of Cook Inlet. Edible berries can be found along the trail.

Trail passes through diverse vegetation: birch–aspen woods, alder-choked gullies, spruce forests, tundra with tiny spruce, mosses, low cranberry bushes, and, finally, hemlock forests with a carpet of moss. Breaks in the woods offer views of the Arm, the shoreline, and Mt. McKinley on clear days. The destination, Gull Rock, protrudes into the water, a good spot for a moment of contemplation.

Do not venture onto the tidal flats. The glacial mud is like quicksand and can trap the unwary hiker, and has led to drowning as the high tide moves in. Be prepared for rapid weather changes.

The trail is closed to mountain bikes at the boundary sign where it crosses into the Kenai National Wildlife Refuge.

Hunting in the area is limited. No fishing opportunities along the trail. Cross-country skiing is possible, though snow conditions are usually poor. Porcupine Campground is the best place for camping because there are no good sites near the trail until the end.

Harding Icefield Trail

3.5 miles   *Kenai Fjords National Park*

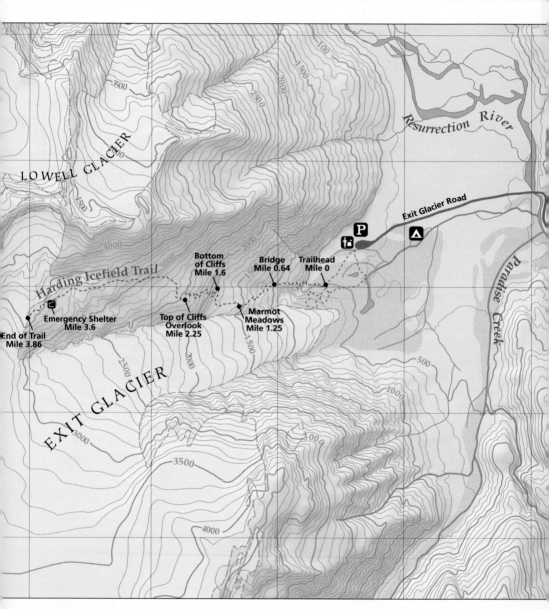

TRAIL INFORMATION

Length One Way: 3.5 miles

Roundtrip Time: 7–8 hours

Recommended Seasons: Summer

Trail End: Harding Icefield

USGS Maps: Seward A-7, A-8

Difficulty: Difficult

Elevation Gain: 2,000 feet

Condition: Fair; snow dependent;
steep muddy sections after rain

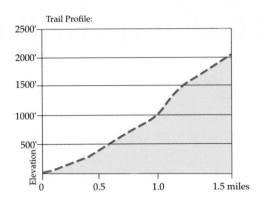

ACCESS

At MP 3.7 of the Seward Highway, turn onto Exit Glacier Road and travel 9 miles to the parking lot. From the parking area, the trailhead is 0.25 miles down a paved trail.

WILDLIFE

Moose, bear, mountain goat, bald eagles, marmot.

DESCRIPTION

Exit Glacier offers an excellent place to see and explore geology, ecology, and wildlife. Short loops offer level hiking with mountain and glacial panoramas. Hike through mature forest stands to alpine tundra. Hikers should take plenty of water, food and warm clothing. During the summer months, park rangers lead daily nature walks to the face of Exit Glacier.

The trail to the icefield is steep with multiple switchbacks. Snow persists into late spring on the lower trail; year-round on the upper trail. The established trail ends with a large cairn midway to the edge of the icefield. Beyond that point, the trail is intermittent and not maintained.

Extreme weather changes can occur—fog, freezing rain, and high winds from the icefield flow down the glacier. Hikers should take care to walk on rocks and snow to avoid trampling the fragile tundra.

Hidden Creek Trail

.65 mile *Kenai National Wildlife Refuge*

HIDDEN LAKE
100
500
Skilak Lake Road
Bear Mountain Trail
Upper Ohmer Lake
Rock Lake
Skilak Lake Road
Hidden Creek Trail
Hidden Creek
SKILAK WILDLIFE RECREATION AREA
1000
Skilak Lookout Trail
x Elev.1568'
SKILAK LAKE

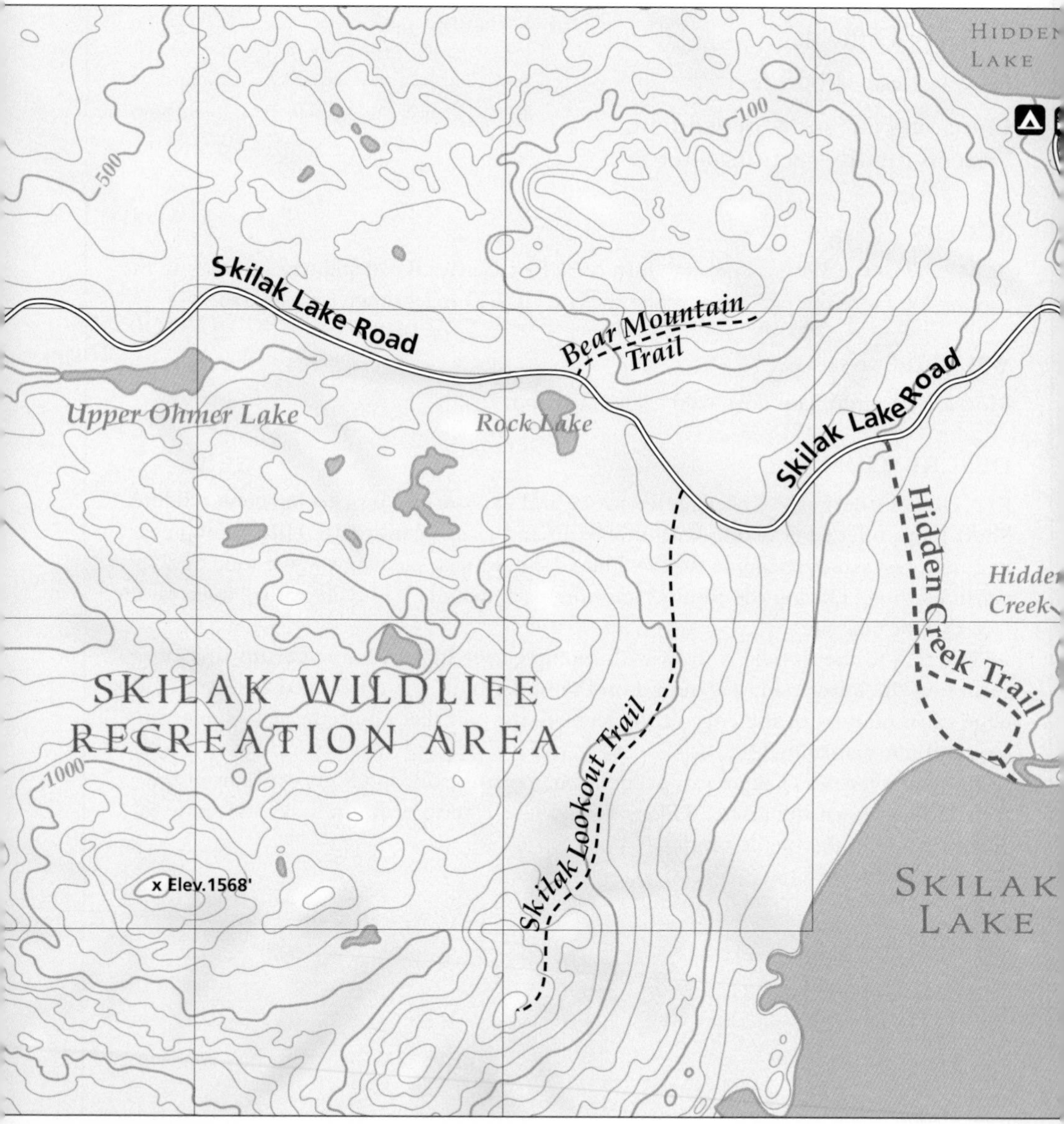

TRAIL INFORMATION

Length One Way: .65 miles

Roundtrip Time: 1.5–2 hours

Recommended Seasons: All seasons

Trail End: Skilak Lake

USGS Map: Kenai B-1

Difficulty: Easy to moderate

Elevation Gain: 300 feet

Condition: Good

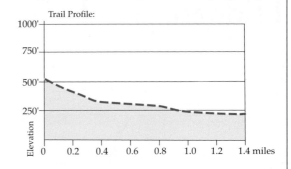

ACCESS

At MP 58 of the Sterling Highway, turn onto Skilak Lake Road. Drive 4.6 miles to the parking area and trailhead. The trailhead is one mile west of Hidden Lake Campground. The parking lot is on the north side of the road and the trail begins on the south side.

WILDLIFE

Moose, black and brown bear, eagles, salmon, river otters, beaver.

DESCRIPTION

This trail provides easy access to Skilak Lake and the mouth of Hidden Creek. The route passes through an area that was burned in May, 1996. The man-made fire burned approximately 5,200 acres. The trail divides about one mile from the trailhead: the west section continues directly to Skilak Lake; the east section heads to Hidden Creek. Both sections join at the lake; the eastern section is about 0.5 mile longer than the western section. You can hike along the beach of Skilak Lake when the water level is low. You'll find excellent views of Kenai Mountains and Skilak Lake at the bottom of the trail. There are undeveloped campsites along Skilak Lake, and the fishing along Skilak Lake and the mouth of Hidden Creek can be fair to good—check fishing regulations before you go. Species include salmon, rainbow and lake trout, and Dolly Varden. Berry picking is good in late summer. Wildlife viewing is also good. The trail provides good cross-country skiing when snow cover is adequate.

    This area can be windy, so bring a sturdy tent. Firewood is available, but stoves are encouraged to reduce human impact. Brown and black bears frequent this trail during Kenai River sockeye salmon runs in June and July.

Hideout Trail

TRAIL INFORMATION

Length One Way: 0.75 mile

Roundtrip Time: 1.5–2 hours

Recommended Seasons: Spring to Fall

Trail End: Rocky Knob overlooking Kenai River and Skilak Lake

USGS Map: Kenai B-1

Difficulty: Moderate in lower section; strenuous in upper section

Elevation Gain: 830 feet

ACCESS

At MP 58 of the Sterling Highway, turn onto Skilak Lake Rd. Drive 1.9 miles to the trailhead. The parking area is on the south side of the road with the trailhead starting across from it on the north side.

WILDLIFE

Moose, black and brown bears, bald eagles.

DESCRIPTION

The trail ascends with a moderate climb giving beautiful views of the Kenai River and Skilak Lake. The last portion from 1,100 to 1,500 feet is much steeper than the beginning to mid-section of the trail. There are nice areas along the many switchbacks of this trail to take photos or eat a picnic lunch. The area was burned during the 1991 Pothole Lake Fire, so it is especially beautiful with fireweed blooming in late July. In August, numerous red elderberry shrubs give color in the fading fireweed blooms.

   The view from the knob is steep and hikers should watch their footing. This trail is a good day hike trail, but does not provide sites or water for backcountry camping.

Johnson Pass Trail

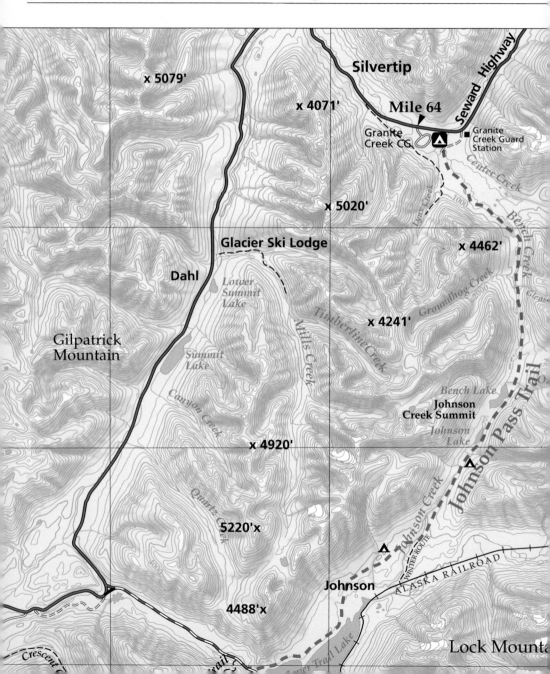

TRAIL INFORMATION

Length One Way: 23 miles

One Way Time: 2–3 days

Recommended Seasons: June–October

Trail End: North or south trailhead

USGS Maps: Seward C-6, C-7

Difficulty: Moderate

Elevation Gain: 1,000 feet

Condition: Well-maintained, though muddy until mid-June

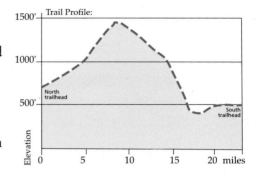

ACCESS

NORTH TRAILHEAD: At MP 64 of the Seward Highway (east of Granite Creek Campground), turn south on the Forest Service signed gravel road for 0.25 mile to trailhead parking.

SOUTH TRAILHEAD: At MP 32.5 Seward Highway, pull into Forest Service signed pullout for trailhead (west of Upper Trail Lake).

Note: Parking areas not plowed in winter. Trail closed to saddle/pack stock from April 1–June 30 and to motorized vehicles from May 1–November 30. Trail closed to motorized vehicles north of Bench Creek all year.

WILDLIFE

Moose, black and brown bear, bald eagles, Dall sheep, and mountain goats

DESCRIPTION

From the north end, the trail climbs through hemlock forests mixed with wetter areas of alder and willow. As the trail levels out, vegetation changes to subalpine with lower-growing shrubs and multitudes of wildflowers. At mile 4, Bench Creek Bridge (a good day hike option for families) the trail enters V-shaped Bench Creek Valley rising up to Bench Lake and into alpine tundra from which you can hike in any direction. Potential campsites in the pass and near the south end of Johnson Lake. Stoves recommended above treeline. Grayling in Bench Lake; rainbow trout in Johnson Lake. From Johnson Lake the trail drops down and then traverses above Upper Trail Lake to the south trailhead.

Good winter ski tour from north trailhead to Bench Creek; from south end to Johnson Pass except during extreme avalanche hazard.

Kenai River Trail

2.8 miles; 2.4 miles   *Kenai National Wildlife Refuge*

TRAIL INFORMATION

Length One Way: 2.8 miles from east trailhead via south river loop;

2.4 miles from west trailhead to river

Roundtrip Time: 2–5 hours, depending on route taken

Recommended Seasons: Late spring, summer and fall

Trail End: Kenai River

USGS Map: Kenai B-1

Difficulty: Easy

Elevation Gain: 250 feet

Condition: Mostly easy to moderate, but steep and slippery near river

ACCESS

AT MP 58 of the Sterling Highway, turn south on Skilak Lake Road. There are two trailheads for this trail. The upper trailhead is 0.6 mile down Skilak Lake Road. West trailhead is 2.3 miles from the eastern Sterling Highway/Skilak Lake Road junction. Upper trail is 2.8 miles; lower trail is 2.4 miles (both one way)

WILDLIFE

Moose, black and brown bear, eagles, waterfowl.

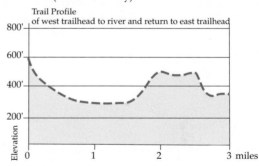

Trail Profile of west trailhead to river and return to east trailhead

DESCRIPTION

From the east trailhead, the trail climbs above the Kenai River canyon and gradually enters boreal forest. After 1.5 miles, the trail divides. The route to the south leads back to the river and follows it downstream where hikers can choose either to continue down the trail until it dead-ends, or complete the loop back to the east or west trailhead. Excellent views of the Kenai River canyon are just a short hike from the east trailhead. Beautiful meadows of wildflowers appear in areas affected by recent fire. Suitable camping areas are available along the river portions of the trail. Firewood is available, but stoves are encouraged to reduce human impact. You can fish for salmon, rainbow trout, and Dolly Varden in the Kenai River. Berry picking is good during the late summer. Both black and brown bear frequent this trail during the June and July sockeye salmon runs.

Snowshoeing opportunities are good in winter. The trail is not well-suited to cross-country skiing.

Lagoon Trail

6.2 miles   *Kachemak Bay State Park*

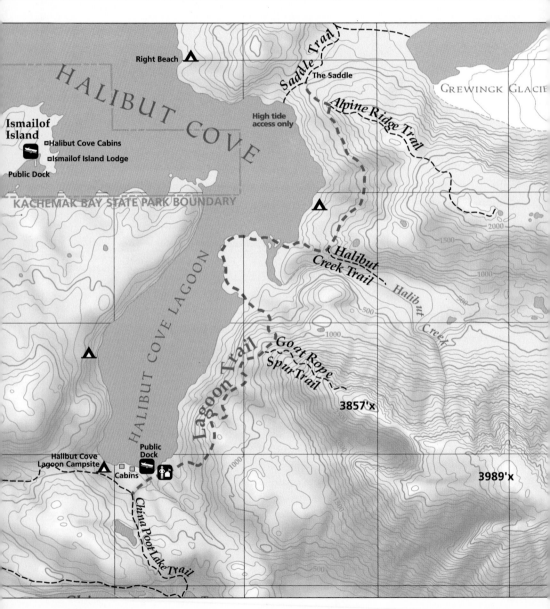

Right Beach

Saddle Trail

The Saddle

GREWINGK GLACIE

HALIBUT COVE

High tide
access only

Alpine Ridge Trail

**Ismailof
Island**

▢Halibut Cove Cabins

▢Ismailof Island Lodge

Public Dock

KACHEMAK BAY STATE PARK BOUNDARY

2000

Halibut
Creek Trail

Halibut Creek

1500

1000

500

HALIBUT COVE LAGOON

1000

Goat Rope
Spur Trail

Lagoon Trail

3857'x

3989'x

1000

Halibut Cove
Lagoon Campsite

Public
Dock

Cabins

China Poot Lake Trail

500

TRAIL INFORMATION

Length One Way: 6.2 miles

Roundtrip Time: 5-7 hours minimum, 1.5 days recommended

Note: This is a rugged, difficult, and exhausting trail. Roundtrips are NOT recommended; hikers who have completed the Lagoon Trail rarely opt to backtrack and rehike it.

Recommended Seasons: Spring, summer

Trail End: South Halibut Cove Lagoon

USGS Maps: Seldovia C-4, C-3, B-4, B-3

Difficulty: Difficult (several long, steep climbs, narrow trail, wet areas, glacial stream crossing)

Elevation Gain: 1,200 feet

Condition: Good

ACCESS

From the north end, use Saddle Trail; from south end, start at Halibut Cove Lagoon Ranger Station.

DESCRIPTION

Lagoon Trail is a challenging, diverse, and primitive route connecting the Grewingk and China Poot areas. From the Saddle Trail, the Lagoon Trail skirts above Halibut Cove, then drops to Halibut Creek Flats. There is no bridge at Halibut Creek. Wade the stream at low tide out on the tidal flats where the water will be shallower—otherwise expect swift, icy, knee- to waist-deep water. Find the trail again by following orange trail markers around the tidal flats. A series of steep switchbacks then climbs into spruce forest to an intersection with Goat Rope Spur Trail, near timberline. The trail continues south, crossing a cascading creek and ends at the ranger station after steep switchbacks. You can camp at Halibut Creek Flats, near the creek crossing, or at the Halibut Cove Lagoon Ranger Station Campsite.

GOAT ROPE SPUR TRAIL (1.5 miles to summit of 3,160 feet) is a short, steep, unmaintained route that begins at the highest point on the Lagoon Trail and leads hikers up to alpine areas. Rock cairns mark the trail to an open alpine ridge, where the trail gently climbs to a summit that has some of the finest views anywhere of Kachemak country. This summit rivals Poot Peak for its views, without the hazardous rocky climbs. Travel beyond the 3,160 foot summit is difficult. Please exercise caution.

Moose Flats
Wetlands Trail

0.25 mile   *Chugach National Forest*

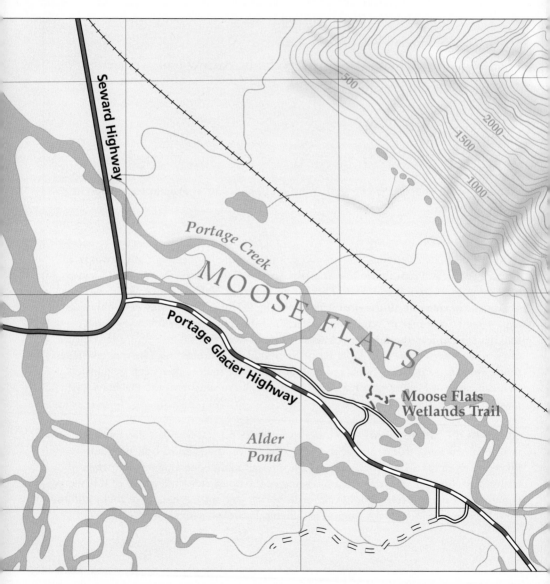

TRAIL INFORMATION

Length One Way: 0.25 mile

Roundtrip Time: 30 minutes

Recommended Seasons: Summer and fall

Trail End: Boardwalk trail begins at Moose Flats Day-Use Area near Willow Ponds and ends in a wetland

USGS Map: Seward D-6

Difficulty: Easy

Elevation Gain: None

Condition: Excellent

ACCESS

Moose Flats Wetland Trail is 1 mile up the Portage Glacier Highway. Park at the Moose Flats Day-Use Area parking lot. Trailhead is beyond the outhouse west of the lakes.

WILDLIFE

Moose, black bear, beaver, bald eagles, and migrating birds. Willow ponds are stocked with trout in early June. Fishermen must be licensed and follow state regulations.

DESCRIPTION

The trail is fully accessible, with sections of packed gravel and elevated boardwalk. There are interpretive signs along the way describing the wetland ecosystem and its inhabitants. This is a good family trail with swimming opportunities. Wildflowers blossom along the trail in summer and you might see moose feeding in the wetlands.

Primrose Trail

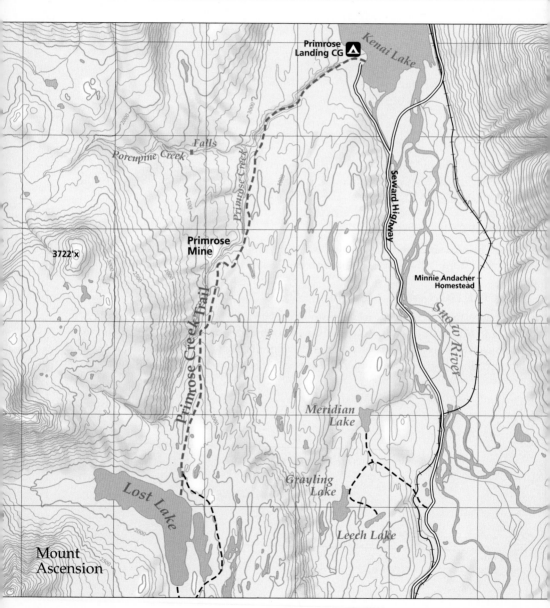

Primrose
Landing CG

Kenai Lake

Porcupine Creek

Falls

Primrose Creek

Seward Highway

Primrose
Mine

3722'x

Minnie Andacher
Homestead

Snow River

Primrose Creek Trail

Meridian
Lake

Grayling
Lake

Lost Lake

Leech Lake

Mount
Ascension

TRAIL INFORMATION

Length One Way: 8 miles

Roundtrip Time: 8-10 hours

Recommended Seasons: All seasons

Trail End: Lost Lake

USGS Map: Seward D-7

Difficulty: More difficult

Elevation Gain: 1,500 feet

Condition: Fair

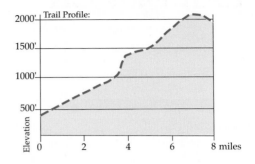

ACCESS

At MP 17 of the Seward Highway, turn northwest and travel 1.5 miles to Primrose Landing Campground. Trailhead is marked in campground. Trail is closed to saddle/pack stock from April 1–June 30 and to motorized vehicles from May 1–November 30. Miner with permit may use motorized vehicle on the trail all year. There is usually snow at higher elevations into mid-June or early July. Bikes are allowed July 1 to March 31.

WILDLIFE

Moose, black bear, mountain goat, Dall sheep, ptarmigan, grouse, marmot.

DESCRIPTION

Excellent multi-day trip to Lost Lake with spectacular scenery. Backcountry campsites near trail and Lost Lake. Excellent area for skiing and snowmobiling in alpine. The first 4.5 miles pass through dense spruce forest. At mile 3, spur trail (steep and unmaintained) leads to viewpoint of Porcupine Creek Falls, a good destination for day hike or family outing. Mining equipment can be seen (on private property) along the trail. The last 2-3 miles are at timberline with dramatic views of mountains and lakes. After reaching timberline, the trail continues to Lost Lake.

Mt. Ascension (5,710 feet) forms the west border of Lost Lake, and requires mountaineering skills to climb to summit. For a view of the steep north side of Mt. Ascension and for increased possibility of seeing black bear and mountain goats, hike along north end of lake and walk west up the valley. For longer cross-country trip, follow drainages to Cooper Lake. Hiking is easy on tundra but good orienteering skills are required. Hunting only in designated seasons. Fishing is good for rainbow trout in Lost Lake.

Winter travel is relatively safe. Whiteouts and disorienting fog may sometimes occur.

Ptarmigan Creek Trail

7.5 miles   *Chugach National Forest*

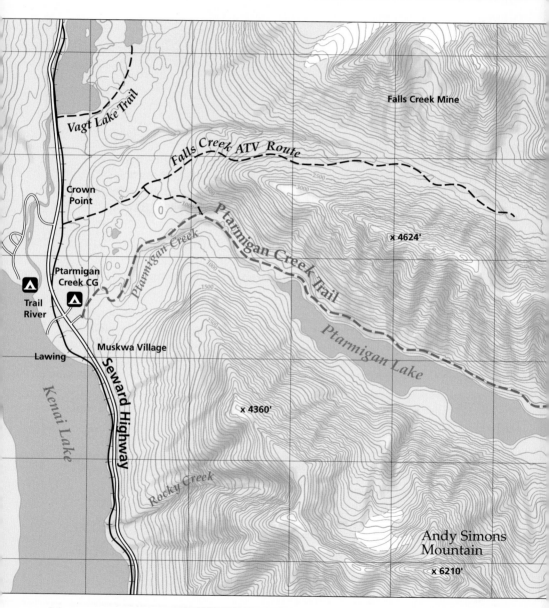

Vagt Lake Trail

Falls Creek Mine

Falls Creek ATV Route

Crown Point

Ptarmigan Creek

Ptarmigan Creek Trail

x 4624'

Ptarmigan Creek CG

Trail River

Ptarmigan Lake

Lawing

Muskwa Village

Seward Highway

Kenai Lake

x 4360'

Rocky Creek

Andy Simons Mountain

x 6210'

TRAIL INFORMATION

Length One Way: 7.5 miles

Roundtrip Time: 6 hours

Recommended Seasons: May–October

Trail End: East end of Ptarmigan Lake

USGS Maps: Seward B-6, B-7

Difficulty: Moderate

Elevation Gain: 450 feet

Condition: Good

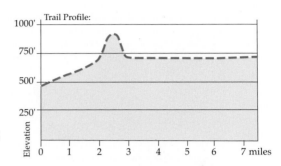

Trail Profile:

ACCESS

At MP 23 of the Seward Highway, turn east into Ptarmigan Creek Campground. Trail begins at south end of campground, and is closed to saddle/pack stock from April 1–June 30 and to motorized vehicles from May 1–November 30. Bikes are allowed July 1 to March 31.

WILDLIFE

Moose, black and brown bear, mountain goats, Dall sheep.

DESCRIPTION

Ptarmigan Creek Trail is suitable for day hikes and multi-day trips with backcountry camping by the lake. Spending the night at the campground and hiking the first two miles of the trail makes a good family outing. From the trailhead, the trail follows the creek upstream. Path is wet in places. Trail leaves spruce forest after mile 2 and ascends through a meadow and back to a wooded area. Many good views of surrounding mountains and alpine areas. Trail continues for 4 miles to east end of lake. There are remains of an old mining cabin on the eastern shore of Ptarmigan Lake. For mountaineering, trail provides access to Andy Simons Mountain south of lake. For a more arduous backcountry trip of 25 to 30 miles, follow old, overgrown unmaintained trail up drainage beyond Ptarmigan Lake, over Snow River Pass to lower Paradise Lake (public recreation cabin at lake). Follow Snow River downstream along remains of Paradise Valley Trail back to railroad and eventually to Seward Highway.

You can hunt in designated seasons. Fish for Dolly Varden and rainbow trout in Ptarmigan Creek and grayling in Ptarmigan Lake. There's excellent viewing of red salmon from campground to mouth of Ptarmigan Creek beginning in late July. Salmon fishing is prohibited in these areas. Trail is unsafe for winter travel.

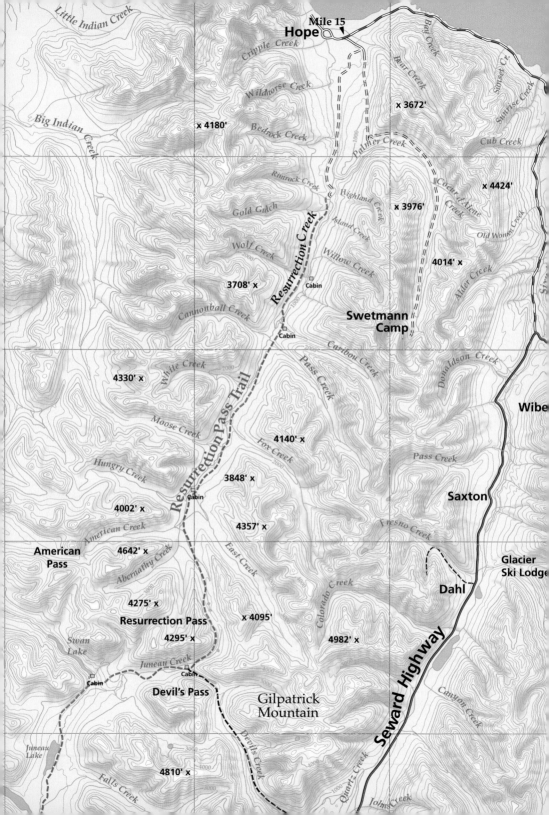

Resurrection Pass Trail
from Hope South to Devil's Pass

21.75 miles   *Chugach National Forest*

TRAIL INFORMATION

Length One Way: 21.75 miles

Roundtrip Time: 2–4 days

Recommended Seasons: All

Trail End: South trailhead

USGS Maps: Seward C-8, D-8

Difficulty: More difficult

Elevation Gain: 2,100 feet

Condition: Good

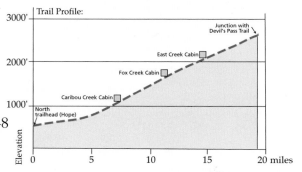

Trail Profile:

ACCESS

Trailhead at MP 15 of the Hope Highway, turn south onto Resurrection Creek Road. Four miles to parking area. Road partially maintained in winter.

WILDLIFE

Moose, black and brown bear, wolves, Dall sheep, mountain goat, grouse.

DESCRIPTION

A mostly level path with gradual grade, but some steep grades with switchbacks. Well maintained, but possibly muddy in spots. Heavy snow near Resurrection Pass persists into late spring. Downed trees can impede travel in winter and spring. There are designated campsites on short spurs off the main route. Popular for hiking, cross-country skiing and snowmobiling. Public recreation cabins at Caribou Creek (mile 7), Fox Creek (mile 11.5) and East Creek (mile 14). Recreational gold panning in designated areas. Spectacular scenery of spruce forest at lower elevations and alpine tundra with wild-flowers. Reddish gray trees along trail were killed by spruce bark beetle. Hunting in designated seasons. Fish for pink salmon in July and August in Resurrection Creek.

    Winter travel is relatively safe, but may also be icy. Travel by snowmobile may be difficult due to narrow trail entering and exiting all drainages between Caribou and East Creek. Trail is hard to follow from East Creek to Resurrection Pass with heavy snowfall. Be prepared for rapid weather changes.

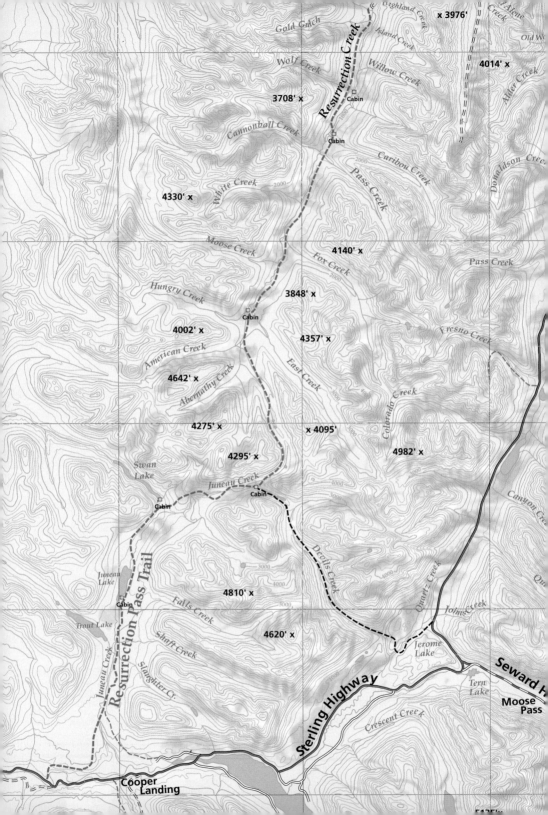

Resurrection Pass Trail
from Cooper Landing North to Devil's Pass

16.75 miles   *Chugach National Forest*

TRAIL INFORMATION

Length One Way: 16.75 miles

Round Trip Time: 2–4 days

Recommended Seasons: All seasons

Trail End: Northern trailhead

USGS Maps: Seward B–8, C–8

Difficulty: More difficult

Elevation Gain: 2,100 feet

Condition: Good

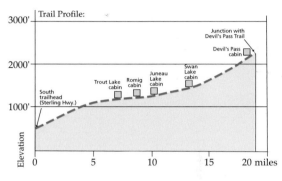

ACCESS

Trailhead at MP 52 of the Sterling Highway, just west of the Russian River Campground. Trail is closed to saddle/pack stock from April 1–June 30 and to motorized vehicles from February 16–November 30. Bikes are allowed July 1 to March 31.

WILDLIFE

Moose, black and brown bear, wolves, Dall sheep, mountain goat, grouse.

DESCRIPTION

There are designated campsites on short spurs off the main route. Trail connects with Devil's Pass Trail for a 28-mile trip to Devils Pass trailhead. Popular for hiking, cross-country skiing, and snowmobiling. Scenic vistas, waterfall, lakes, and streams. Day hike to Juneau Falls, 4.5 miles from trailhead. Public recreation cabins at Trout Lake (mile 7), Romig (mile 9), Juneau Lake (mile 9.5), Swan Lake (mile 13), and Pass (mile 18) from trailhead.

You can fish in Juneau Creek for Dolly Varden, rainbow trout and grayling. In Trout Lake, fish for whitefish, rainbow trout, and lake trout. In Juneau Lake, you'll find whitefish, burbot, grayling, rainbow trout, and lake trout. In Swan Lake are Dolly Varden, sockeye salmon, and rainbow trout.

Russian Lakes Trail

21 miles   *Chugach National Forest*

Russian River CG

Mile 52   **Sterling Highway**   Mile 48

Schooner Bend

Gwin's Lodge

Cooper Landing

Snug Harbor

Snug Harbor Road

Russian Mountain

Lower Russian Lake

Barber Cabin

Russian Lakes Trail

Cooper Creek

Stetson Creek Trail

Stetson Creek

Rhode Mountain

KENAI LA

4465'x

5060'x

4147'x

4625'x

3449'x

Cooper Mountain

5270'x

COOPER LAKE

Cooper Lake R

Pothole Lake

Aspen Flats Cabin

Upper Russian Lake Cabin

Upper Russian Lake

Russian Lakes Trail

TRAIL INFORMATION

Length One Way: 21 miles

Roundtrip Time: 2-4 days

Recommended Season: North end: May-Oct.; South end: all seasons

Trail End: East or west trailhead (see Access below)

USGS Maps: Seward B-8,
Kenai B-1

Difficulty: Easy (summer);
More difficult (winter)

Elevation Gain: 1,100 feet

Condition: Excellent

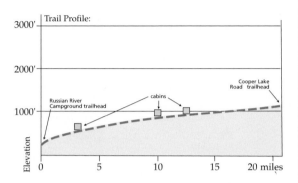

Trail Profile:

3000'

2000'

1000'

Cooper Lake
Road trailhead

cabins

Russian River
Campground trailhead

Elevation

0   5   10   15   20 miles

ACCESS

WEST TRAILHEAD: At MP 52 of the Sterling Highway, turn onto Russian River
Campground Road. One mile to trailhead parking. EAST TRAILHEAD: At MP 48 of
the Sterling Highway, turn on Snug Harbor Road. Travel nine miles to Cooper Lake
Road. Three miles to parking area. Cooper Lake Road is not plowed in winter. Snug
Harbor Road may be icy. Bikes are allowed July 1 to March 31. Snowmobiles (except
for subsistence) are not allowed from the Lower Russian Lake Trailhead to Aspen Flats
cabin year-round, this includes the Barber Cabin Trail.

DESCRIPTION

The trail has gradual grades, and is well maintained. There are designated campsites at
Lower and Upper Russian lakes and on short spurs off the main trail. There are three
public recreation cabins on the trail. Day hike from Russian River Campground to
Russian River Falls (mile 2) or Lower Russian Lake (mile 3). First three miles of trail are
heavily used for fishing access to Russian River and Lower Russian Lake. Along the trail,
reddish-gray, dead trees (a major fire hazard) were killed by spruce bark beetle. Hunting
allowed in designated seasons. Russian River is the largest sport fishery in Alaska for
sockeye salmon. Excellent rainbow trout fishing in and between Upper and Lower
Russian lakes. No salmon fishing permitted upstream of Russian River Falls.

Snow on trail can persist into late spring. Downed trees can impede travel in
winter/spring. Severe avalanche danger in winter at Lower Russian Lake. Relatively safe
from Cooper Lake trailhead except during extreme avalanche hazard. Trail is closed to
saddle/pack stock from April 1 to June 30 and to motorized vehicles from May 1 to
November 30. Parking fee for trailhead parking.

Saddle Trail

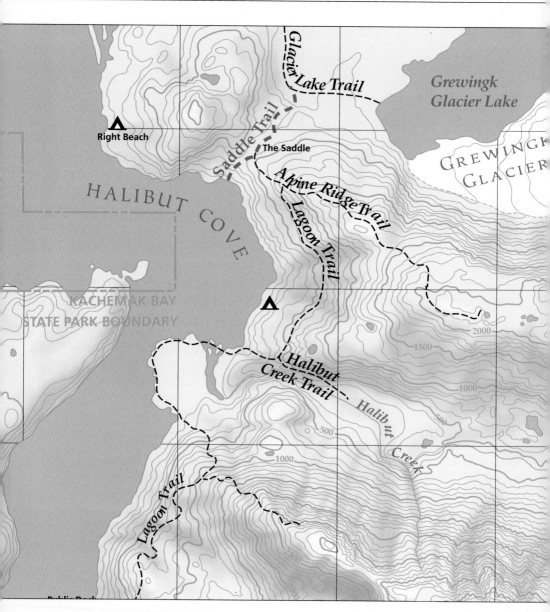

Glacier Lake Trail

Grewingk Glacier Lake

Saddle Trail

Right Beach

The Saddle

GREWINGK GLACIER

Alpine Ridge Trail

HALIBUT COVE

Lagoon Trail

KACHEMAK BAY STATE PARK BOUNDARY

Halibut Creek Trail

Halibut Creek

2000

1500

1000

500

500

1000

Lagoon Trail

2500

Public Beach

52

TRAIL INFORMATION

Length One Way: 1 mile

Roundtrip Time: 25 minutes

Recommended Seasons: Spring and summer

Trail End: Glacier Lake Trail

USGS Maps: Seldovia C-4, C-3, B-4, B-3

Difficulty: Moderate with short, steep climbs

Elevation Gain: 350 feet

Condition: Good

ACCESS

Boat or floatplane access only to Kachemak Bay State Park; Marine access (tide dependent) at Halibut Cove (protected anchorage, mooring buoys). Good afternoon pickup spot.

WILDLIFE

Moose, black bear, mountain goats, coyotes, and wolves. Bald eagles, gyrfalcons, and puffins.

DESCRIPTION

No campsites at trailhead, but you can camp at Grewingk Glacier Lake sites. The trail leads you over a low ridge between Halibut Cove and Grewingk Glacier. The trail switchbacks through steep, forested terrain, and it accesses the Alpine Ridge and Lagoon trails. Cliffs prohibit hiking the beach from the trailhead in the Right Beach Campsite—boat transport is necessary.

Short Hikes near Seward

All less than 2 miles   Chugach National Forest

Primrose Mine

Minnie Andacher Homestead

Snow River

Seward Highway

Primrose Creek Trail

2000

1300

Meridian Lake

Grayling Lake

Leech Lake

Lost Lake

▶ **Mile 13.2**

TRAIL INFORMATION

Length One Way: See each hike. All less than 2 miles

Recommended Seasons: All seasons

USGS Map: Seward B-7

Difficulty: Easy

Elevation Gain: Minimal

Condition: Good

ACCESS

Grayling Lake trailhead is located at MP 13.2 of the Seward Highway, with parking for about 14 cars.

WILDLIFE

Moose, black and brown bear, mountain goat, ptarmigan, grouse.

DESCRIPTION

GRAYLING LAKE TRAIL is a 2-mile route in good condition with gradual elevation gains. An excellent family trail that passes through spruce forests and open meadows. Grayling fishing.

MERIDIAN LAKE TRAIL is 1.75 miles up the Grayling Lake Trail. This short spur angler's trail leads to Meridian Lake.

LEECH LAKE TRAIL begins 0.5-miles along the angler's access trail to Leech Lake and is found along the eastern shore of Grayling Lake.

Also, GOLDEN FIN LAKE TRAIL (not shown) begins at MP 11.6 of the Seward Highway. The trail is 0.6 miles long, and with its gradual elevation gain makes a good family trail. The trail passes through open meadows, bogs, hemlock forests, and a pond of lilies. Berry picking opportunities are good in mid- to late August. Sturdy, waterproof boots are recommended. When snowfall is sufficient, area offers good sledding and skiing.

Skilak Lookout Trail

2 miles *Kenai National Wildlife Refuge*

Hidden Lake
100
500
Skilak Lake Road
Bear Mountain Trail
Upper Ohmer Lake
Rock Lake
Skilak Lake Road
Hidden Creek Trail
500
SKILAK WILDLIFE
RECREATION AREA
100
Skilak Lookout Trail
X 1568'
Skilak Lake

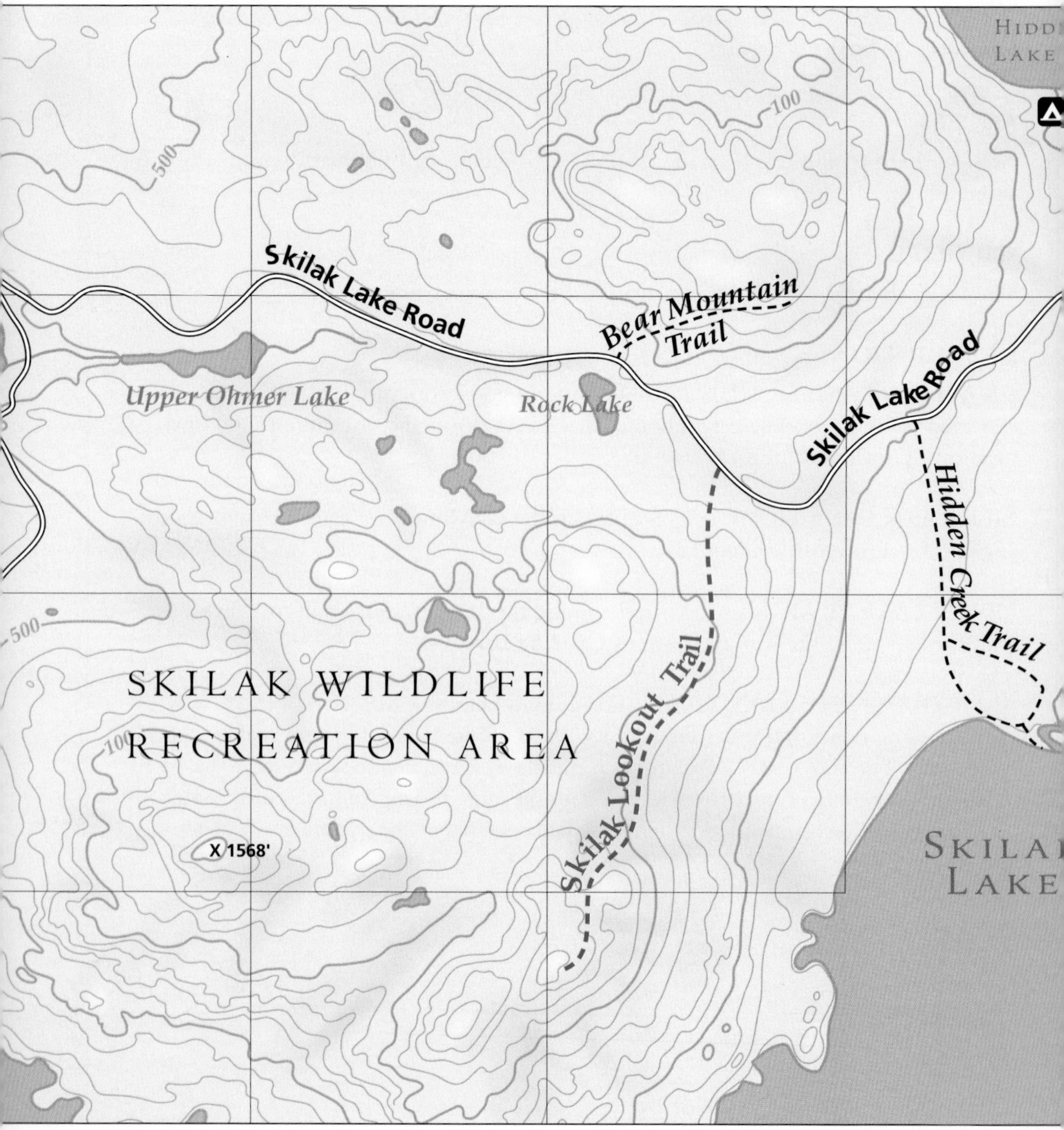

TRAIL INFORMATION

Length One Way: 2 miles

Roundtrip Times: 3–4 hours

Recommended Season: All seasons

Trail End: Skilak Lookout

USGS Map: Kenai B-1

Difficulty: Moderate

Elevation Gain: 700 feet

Condition: Good

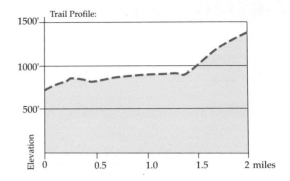

Trail Profile:

ACCESS

At MP 58 of the Sterling Highway, turn onto Skilak Lake Road. Drive 5.5 miles to the parking area on the north side of road; trailhead is on south side of road.

WILDLIFE

Black and brown bear, moose.

DESCRIPTION

Trail passes through boreal forest, which burned during the Hidden Creek Fire in 1996. The trail ends atop a knob overlooking Skilak Lake. View at the end of the trail is spectacular—Skilak Lake, Kenai Mountains, and the Kenai River. Don't forget your camera! Few areas are suitable for camping. Look for bear and moose. Many species of wildflowers can be seen throughout the summer. Good snowshoeing area.

Sturdy hiking boots are recommended. Water is not available during most of the summer. Bears frequent this trail from late July to mid-September when berries and mountain ash fruit are ripe.

Skyline Trail

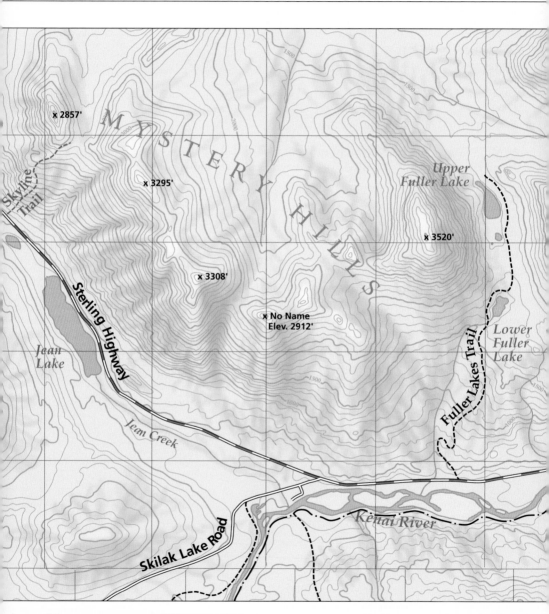

x 2857'

M Y S T E R Y   H I L L S

x 3295'

Skyline Trail

x 3308'

Upper
Fuller Lake

x 3520'

x No Name
Elev. 2912'

Sterling Highway

Jean
Lake

Lower
Fuller
Lake

Fuller Lakes Trail

Jean Creek

Skilak Lake Road

Kenai River

TRAIL INFORMATION

Length One Way: 1 mile

Roundtrip Time: 3-5 hours

Recommended Seasons: Spring-Fall

Trail End: Peak of the Mystery Hills

USGS Maps: Kenai B-1, C-1

Difficulty: Strenuous

Elevation Gain: 1,800 feet

Condition: Steep, rocky, slippery on rainy days

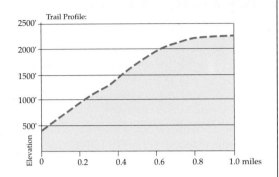

ACCESS

The Skyline Trail is at MP 61 of the Sterling Highway; trailhead on north side, parking is on the south side.

WILDLIFE

Moose, black and brown bear, Dall sheep, ptarmigan, grouse, songbirds.

DESCRIPTION

Skyline Trail rises from boreal forest to above treeline in the first 0.75 miles. The route gives you quick access to the mountains in the Mystery Creek Unit. The trail ends in an alpine saddle, with off-trail hikes possible to the nearby peaks. Wildflowers abound in this alpine area throughout the summer. There are no established campsites, but a few suitable areas are available off the trail. There's good berry picking in late summer. Firewood is not available above treeline, so stoves are necessary. After snow melts, little water is available. Winter use is not recommended due to steepness and possibility of avalanches.

Trail Users Guide

LEAVE NO TRACE

As more people come to Alaska to experience its special beauty, the chances of damaging valuable resources and impacting wilderness increase. We ask that you take an active part in protecting the quality of our natural areas, so others may continue to enjoy them. Here are a few suggestions on how you can help.

LITTER Please pack out what you pack in. This includes food, packaging, old fishing gear, diapers—EVERYTHING that you brought with you.

HUMAN WASTE Burying human waste at least 200 feet from water sources, trails, and camps will assure proper sanitation in the backcountry. Carefully remove surface duff, dig a hole several inches into the soil, and put all human waste into the hole. Pack toilet paper out with your trash.

FIRES To reduce the chance of wildfires and number of fire scars, the use of a lightweight backpacking stove is highly recommended. If you need to start a camp-fire, please keep it small. Burn only dead and downed wood. Use an established fire ring or build a mound fire. Extinguish fires completely and pack out all the trash from your fire.

CAMP LOCATIONS Where you camp is very important. Here are a few tips. Camp at least 200 feet from water sources to prevent contamination. Stay out of sight and earshot of trails. Use an existing site, if available. If you are on an off-trail trip, change camping locations every couple of days to prevent heavy impact on the vegetation. Do not trench around tents or erect structures (benches, tables, etc.). Do not camp near public recreation cabins.

BE PREPARED

Trekking into the backcountry of the Kenai Peninsula can be a great way to see Alaska's wildlife, experience solitude, and enjoy magnificent vistas. A pleasant outing is usually dependent on knowledge, thorough preparation and good judgment. The following tips will help get you ready.

CLOTHING Even in the summer, it can be wet and windy with temperatures in the 40s (Farenheit), and colder at higher elevations. Be prepared for unexpected weather changes. Help prevent hypothermia by packing the following items:

> Layered clothing (wool and synthetics that keep you warm when wet)
>
> Sturdy hiking boots and light shoes for around camp
>
> Good quality rain gear: hooded coat and rain pants
>
> Hat (for sun and cold), extra socks, and gloves

FIRST AID/SURVIVAL Include the following first aid/survival items:

> First aid kit
>
> Matches/lighter
>
> Emergency blanket
>
> Map and compass
>
> Knife
>
> Signalling device

FOOD Hiking is a high-energy activity, so bring lightweight foods rich in carbohydrates: fruits, nuts, cheese, crackers, and peanut butter.

WATER Natural water sources are unavailable on some trails. Bring water with you, and drink often to avoid dehydration. If surface water is available, we recommend purification by using an appropriately rated water filter.

WILDLIFE Black and brown bears are common in most areas of the Kenai peninsula. They can be dangerous. Follow a few simple rules: make noise while hiking; avoid bringing anything with a strong odor. Stay alert. Stay away from bear trails and other areas frequented by bears. At night, tie food and garbage in several sealed plastic bags 20 feet high and 200 feet away from your camp, or use bear-proof containers. Moose can also be dangerous, so give them plenty of room. Don't forget the little critters, too. Insects—particularly mosquitoes—can be overwhelming at times. Bring insect repellent and a head net.

PUBLIC RECREATION CABINS 17 national forest public use cabins are available for a fee on the Chugach National Forest portion of the Kenai Peninsula. Cabins are located on lakes, streams, trails, and in mountain valleys.

Most cabins are about 12 feet by 14 feet and have wood or oil stoves. Furnishings include a table, chairs, and wooden bunks for four or more people Bring your own food, sleeping bag, pad, and oil for cabins with oil stoves. Each cabin has its own outhouse and some cabins on lakes have rowboats. The National Forest Service is remodeling existing cabins so they will be accessible to people with disabilities.

Cabins that are not used as frequently as others and some cabins during the winter may be reserved for up to seven consecutive nights. Popular cabins may be reserved for up to three consecutive nights during high-use periods.

All cabins must be reserved and the cabin fee paid in advance. Cabins may be reserved up to 179 days in advance of the first day of occupancy. Fees vary per cabin, averaging between $25-$45, but are subject to change. Check with the Chugach Forest Service office, USFS Reservation Center (877) 444-6777 or ReserveUSA.com or the Alaska Public Lands Information Center in Anchorage for current rates, information, and reservations.

For More Information

Chugach National Forest
Supervisor's Office
3301 C Street, Suite 300
Anchorage, Alaska 99503
(907) 743-9500
www.fs.fed.us/r10/chugach/

Kenai Fjords National Park
P.O. Box 1727
Seward, Alaska 99664
(907) 224-3175
www.nps.gov/kefj/

Kenai National Wildlife Refuge
P.O. Box 2139
Soldotna, Alaska 99669
(907) 262-7021
http://kenai.fws.gov/

Alaska Public Lands Information Center
605 West Fourth Avenue, Suite 105
Anchorage, Alaska 99501
(907) 271-2737
www.nps.gov/aplic/center/

Alaska Natural History Association
750 West Second Ave., Suite 100
Anchorage, Alaska 99501
(907) 274-8440
www.alaskanha.org

Notes: